MW00635476

the DMC
BOOK OF
charted
TATTING DESIGNS

designs by
Kirstine Nikolajsen &
Inge Lise Nikolajsen

LACIS
PUBLICATIONS

This book is meant as a help for those who love to tat but find it difficult to follow the written patterns.

Kirstine Nikolajsen & Inge Lise Nikolajsen
Tommerup, August 1993

PUBLISHER'S NOTES

The graphic presentation of tatting patterns would seem quite logical, considering the clarity of organization of the finished work. By looking at the charted pattern the tatter can see instantly the structure, the starting point and the direction of the work. It is much like using a road map to get from point A to point B rather than a description by words only.

With the diagrams understood it will soon be a simple matter to translate any finished tatting design to a corresponding diagram for reproduction and it will certainly facilitate the creation of your own designs in translating a sketch to an original tatted piece.

While this text gives full instructions for shuttle tatting, the charted patterns are equally relevant to *NEEDLE TATTING*, which has become an alternate and preferred method by many tatters.

LACIS
1998

Translated from the original Danish book
ORKIS, published in 1994
by FORLAGET NOTABENE
ISBN 87-7490-323-3
© Kristine Nikolajsen & Inge Lise Nikolajsen

This English language edition published by
LACIS PUBLICATIONS
3163 Adeline Street
Berkeley, CA 94703

© 1998, Lacis
ISBN 1-891656-06-6

Produced for
the DMC Corporation
South Hackensack Avenue
Port Kearny, Bldg. 10A
South Kearny, NJ 07032-4688

CONTENTS

MATERIALS

Two or more SHUTTLES (preferably in different colors).

A fine CROCHET HOOK: to make joinings.

A small pair of TWEEZERS: to open rings (if there should be a mistake!).

A PAPER CLIP: Used in some designs at the beginning of the work and to make space in a chain.

THREAD: Hard and smooth so it slides easily through the knots. The thread can be made of cotton, flax or silk. The designs shown are tatted from DMC Tatting Thread, DMC Pearl Cotton, DMC *Cordonnet* or DMC *Cebelia* crochet thread in different thicknesses and different colors.

WORKING NOTES

Each design is presented as a visual pattern and illustrated by a photograph.

Charted patterns are a new method of conveying directions in tatting. These visual diagrams are much easier to use, and convey working instructions more clearly than a written text.

The diagrams often show only parts of the pattern: i.e. only one or more motifs which are then to be repeated and joined. Each diagram is accompanied by a photo that shows the result of the work.

When necessary for clarity, working notes have been added.

The material used for each model is noted as is the size of the finished work. If alternate materials are used the finished size will vary unless adjustment in stitch count is made.

Where two shuttles are used, it is easier if they have different colors or are individually marked such as "1" and "2". The second shuttle is always the ball thread.

Where " + ball thread" is specified, you can use either the thread directly from the ball or the thread from a second shuttle.

REMEMBER: Study the diagram, the photo and the explanation of the symbols carefully before you start tatting!

EXPLANATION OF SYMBOLS

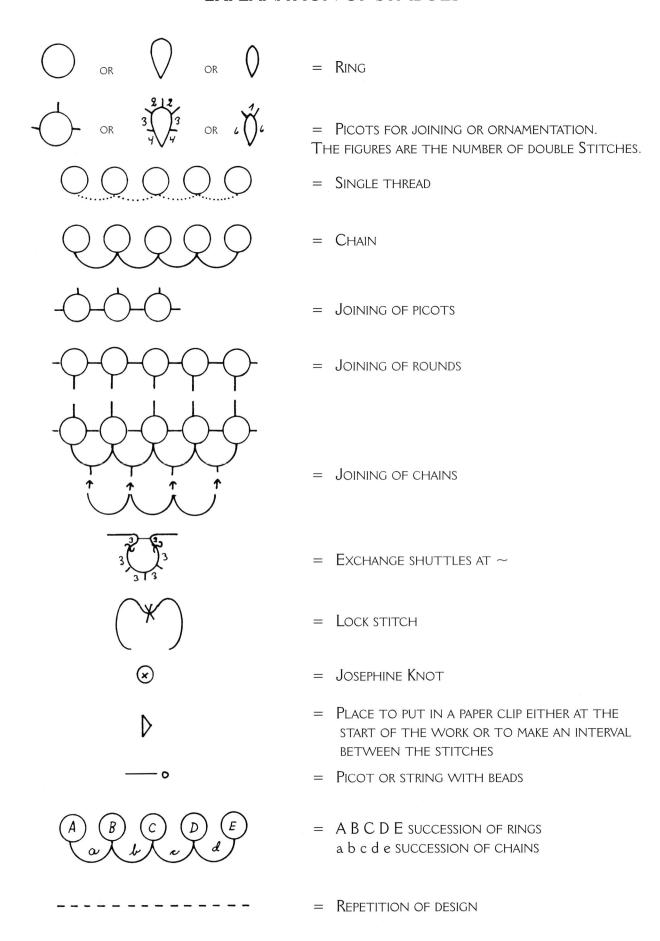

OR   OR   = RING

OR   OR   = PICOTS FOR JOINING OR ORNAMENTATION.
THE FIGURES ARE THE NUMBER OF DOUBLE STITCHES.

= SINGLE THREAD

= CHAIN

= JOINING OF PICOTS

= JOINING OF ROUNDS

= JOINING OF CHAINS

= EXCHANGE SHUTTLES AT ~

= LOCK STITCH

= JOSEPHINE KNOT

= PLACE TO PUT IN A PAPER CLIP EITHER AT THE
START OF THE WORK OR TO MAKE AN INTERVAL
BETWEEN THE STITCHES

= PICOT OR STRING WITH BEADS

= A B C D E SUCCESSION OF RINGS
a b c d e SUCCESSION OF CHAINS

= REPETITION OF DESIGN

TECHNIQUE

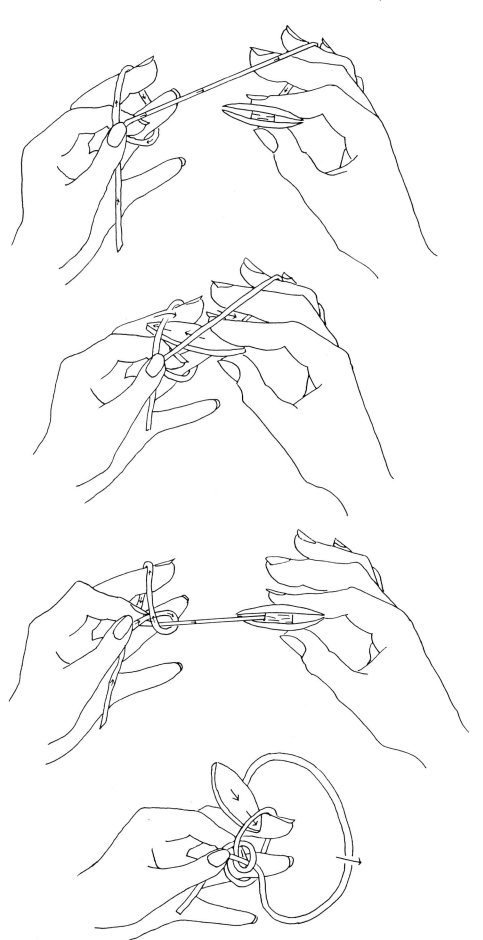

The technique is very simple. There is only one knot or rather two half knots: *left half* and *right half*. Together they make a *double stitch*.

THE LEFT HALF OF THE KNOT:

Figure 1

Place the thread around the left hand fingertips and keep it firm with thumb and forefinger.

Figure 2

Make a loop with the shuttle under the left hand thread.

Figure 3

Release the grip in the left hand and pull the shuttle. This makes the loop transfer to the other thread.

THE RIGHT HALF OF THE KNOT:

Figure 4:

Make a loop with the shuttle over the left hand thread. Release the grip in the left hand and pull the shuttle in the same way as in left half of the knot.

Figure 5: Picot

A picot is a shorter or longer space between two double stitches and is used for ornamentation and joining.

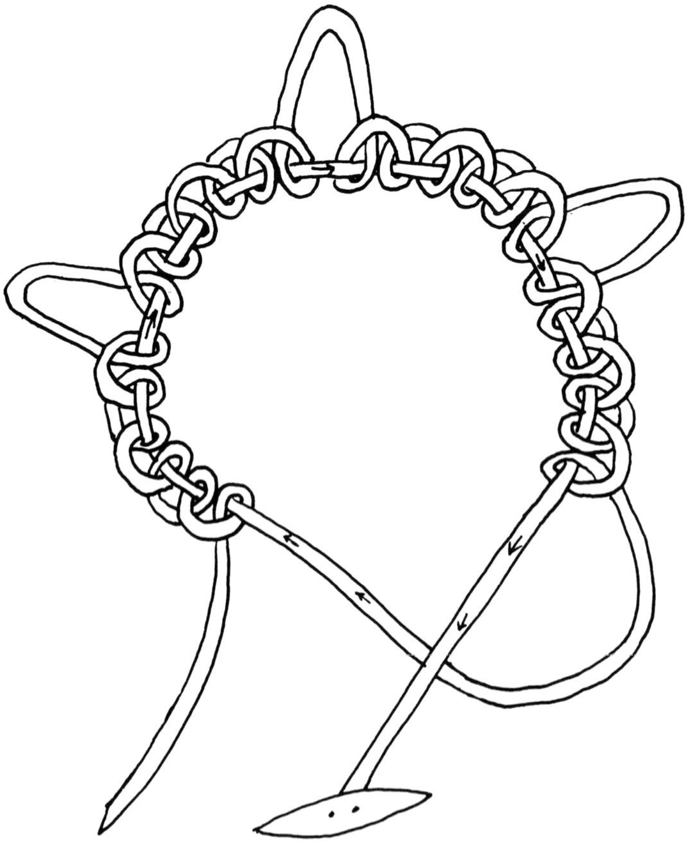

Figure 6: To Close a Ring

When the wanted number of stitches have been made, pull them together to form a ring.

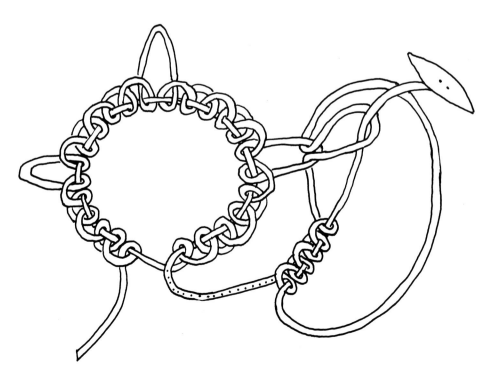

Figure 7: Joining Rings

Pull the thread though a picot with use of a crochet hook.

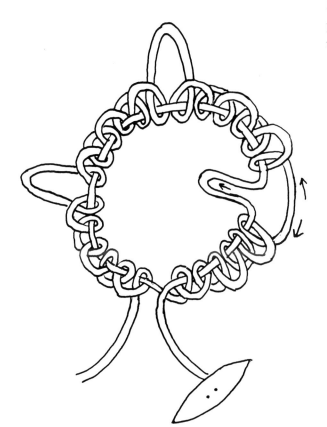

Figure 8: The Opening of a Ring

It is possible to open a ring at a picot and then to pull the inner thread with a pair of tweezers.

Figure 9: Sample with Rings

Joined rings tatted with one shuttle.

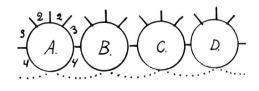

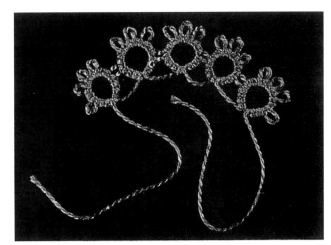

Figure 10: Sample with Rings

Joined rings tatted with one shuttle. The work is turned between each ring.

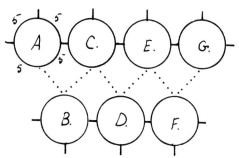

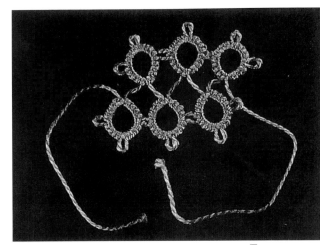

Figure 11: Chains

Chains are made with the thread either from the ball or from the second shuttle. Turn the work when the ring is tatted, and tat the chain with the ball thread.

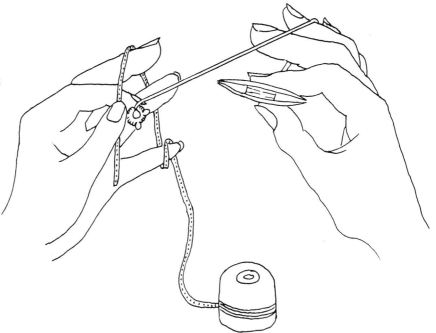

Figure 12: Sample with Ball Thread

Tatted with one shuttle and ball thread.

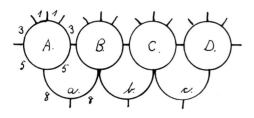

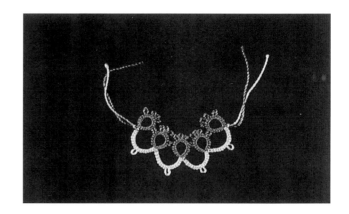

Figure 13: Sample with Rings on Chains

The chain (a) is interrupted by the ring (B). The ring is tatted with the thread from the second shuttle.

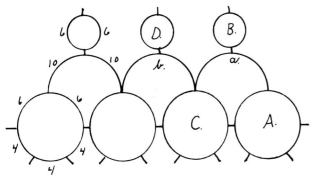

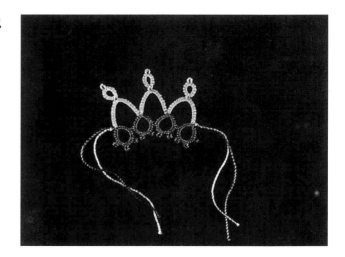

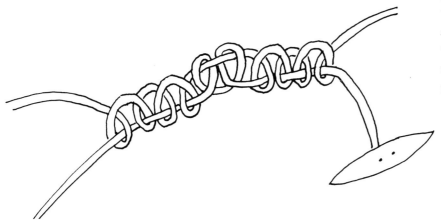

Figure 14: Lock Stitch

A lock stitch is a double stitch where the loops are made with the shuttle, i.e. the stitch locks the work and can't be pulled.

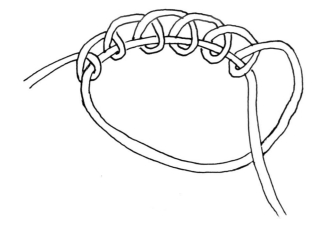

Figure 15: Josephine Knot

A Josephine knot is made of *half stitches* pulled together. The result is a spiraling knot.

Figure 16: Renewing a Thread

When the thread needs to be renewed, tie the ends together very close to the ring. Place the ends along the inner thread. Make 3-4 stitches and cut off the ends.

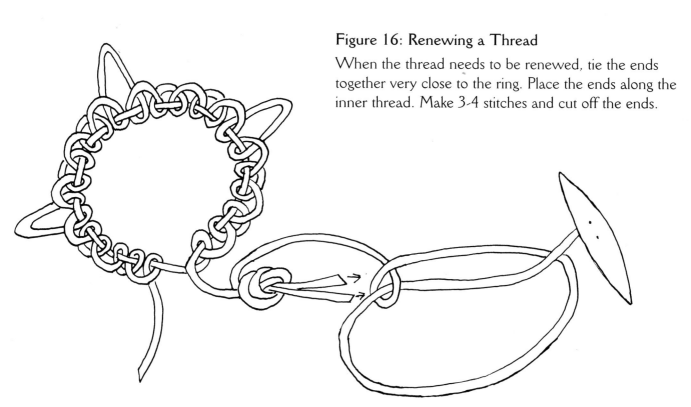

Figure 17: Fastening of Ends at a Closed Ring

Place a paper clip around the starting thread and use a hook to lead the thread end through the first double stitches.

At the end place a thin doubled thread into the last double stitches.

Close the ring as usual and cut the thread. Remove the paper clip and tie the ending thread to this loop. Pull the loop tight and, by use of the inlayed thread, pull the ending thread back through the last stitches.

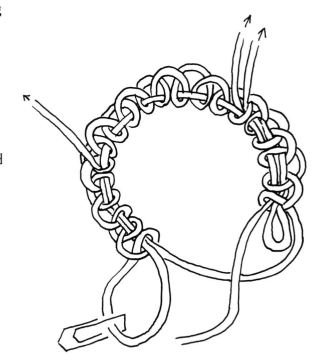

Figure 18: Fastening of Ends at End of Round

Place a paper clip at the start of the work.

Place a normal doubled thread into the last four stitches and a thin doubled sewing thread into the last three stitches.

Cut the thread, remove paper clip, pull one of the thread ends through the small loop at the

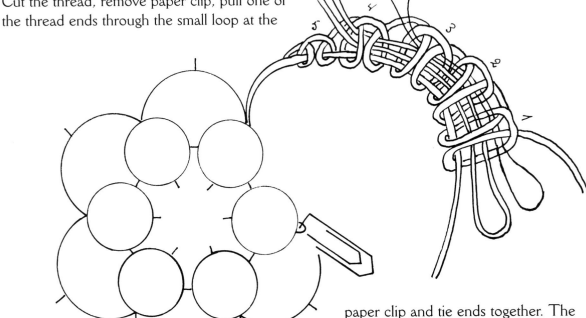

paper clip and tie ends together. The thread ends are pulled back into the stitches by use of the inlayed threads. The thick thread is pulled out first.

10

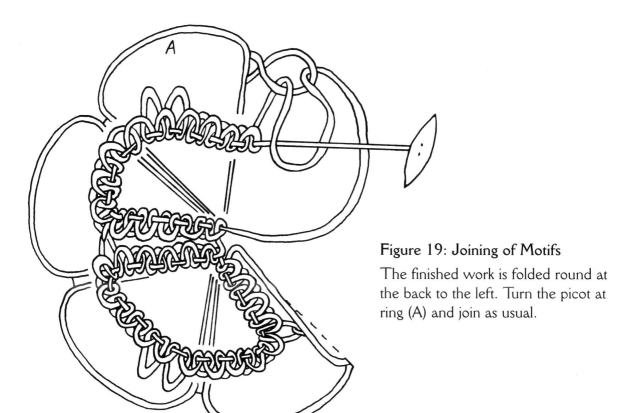

Figure 19: Joining of Motifs

The finished work is folded round at the back to the left. Turn the picot at ring (A) and join as usual.

Figure 20: Drawing of Lace Corner

A corner can be joined to a straight lace by use of a mirror. Place the mirror at the lace so the lace in the mirror is seen at a right angle. Move the mirror until it is technically possible to tat the appearing corner.

No 1: SQUARE MOTIF

Material:	1 shuttle
Thread:	DMC Cordonnet No. 50
Size:	Width 4 cm

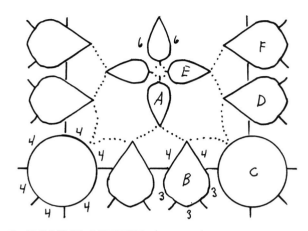

No 2: ROUND MOTIF

Material:	1 shuttle + ball thread
Thread:	DMC Cordonnet No. 50
Size:	Diameter 5 cm

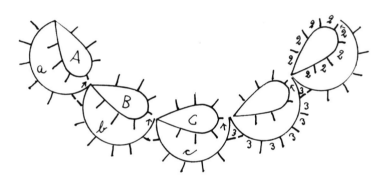

No 3: ROUND MOTIF

Material:	1 shuttle + ball thread
Thread:	DMC Cordonnet No. 50
Size:	Diameter 5 cm

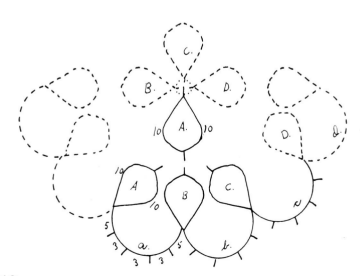

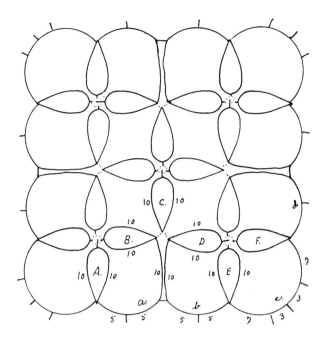

No 4: SQUARE MOTIF

Material: 1 shuttle + ball thread
Thread: DMC Cordonnet No. 50
Size: Width 5 cm

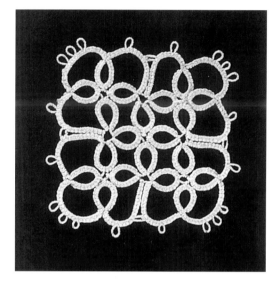

No 5: ROUND MOTIF

Material: 1 shuttle
Thread: DMC Cordonnet No. 50
Size: Diameter 5.5 cm

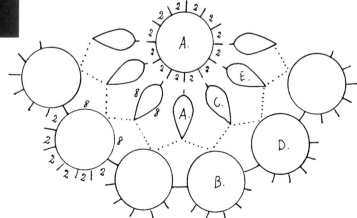

No 6: ROUND MOTIF

Material: 1 shuttle + ball thread to last row
Thread: DMC Cordonnet No. 50
Size: Diameter 7.5 cm

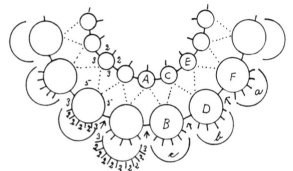

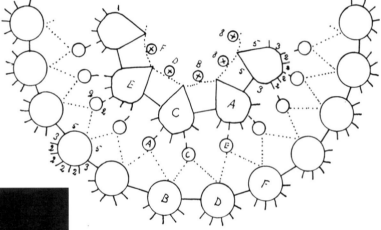

No 7: ROUND MOTIF

Material: 1 shuttle
Thread: DMC Cordonnet No. 50
Size: Diameter 8 cm

No 8: OCTAGONAL MOTIF

Material: 2 shuttles
Thread: DMC Cordonnet No. 40
Size: Diameter 8 cm

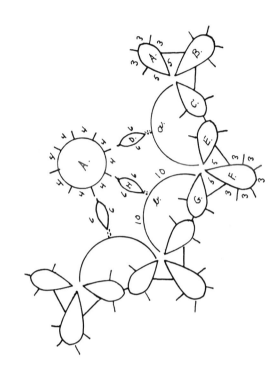

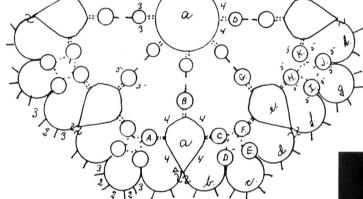

No 9: OCTAGONAL MOTIF

The innermost ring (a) is a chain tatted with ball thread. Start with 2 double stitches and end with 2 double stitches.

2nd round is started with a paper clip at chain (a) which is tatted with the ball thread.

Material: 2 shuttles
Thread: DMC Cordonnet No. 50
Size: Diameter 7 cm

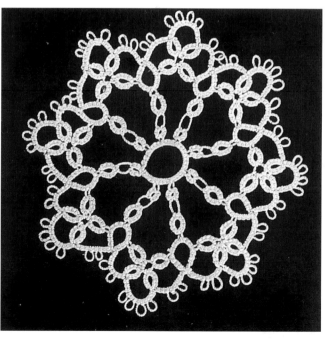

No 10: LACE WITH CORNER

Material: 1 shuttle
Thread: DMC Cordonnet No. 70
Size: Width 2 cm

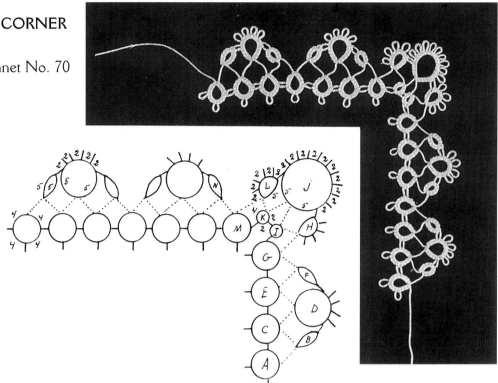

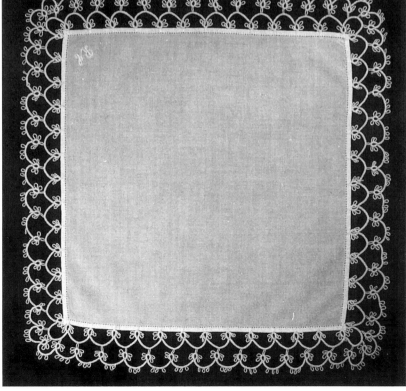

No 11: LACE WITH CORNER

The lace is tatted directly on a ready-made handkerchief.

Material: 1 shuttle + ball thread
Thread: DMC Cordonnet No. 70
Size: Width 2.5 cm

No 12: LACE WITH CORNER

Material: 2 shuttles
Thread: DMC Cordonnet No. 70
Size: Width 1.5 cm

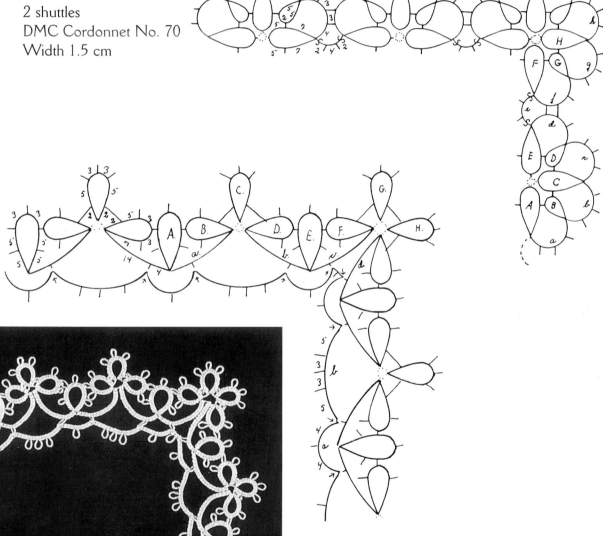

No 13: LACE WITH CORNER

Material: 1 shuttle + ball thread
Thread: DMC Cordonnet No. 70
Size: Width 2.5 cm

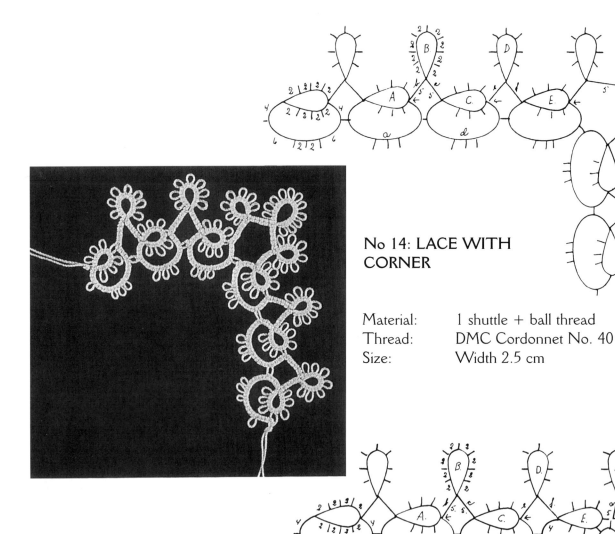

No 14: LACE WITH CORNER

Material: 1 shuttle + ball thread
Thread: DMC Cordonnet No. 40
Size: Width 2.5 cm

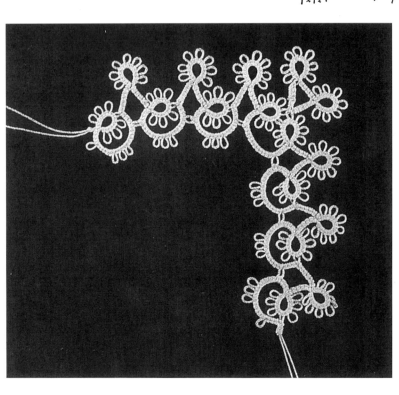

No 15: LACE WITH CORNER

The lace is the same as no. 14 except for the corner.

Notice that the corner motif is tatted on at the end.

Material: 1 shuttle + ball thread
Thread: DMC Cordonnet No. 40
Size: Width 2.5 cm

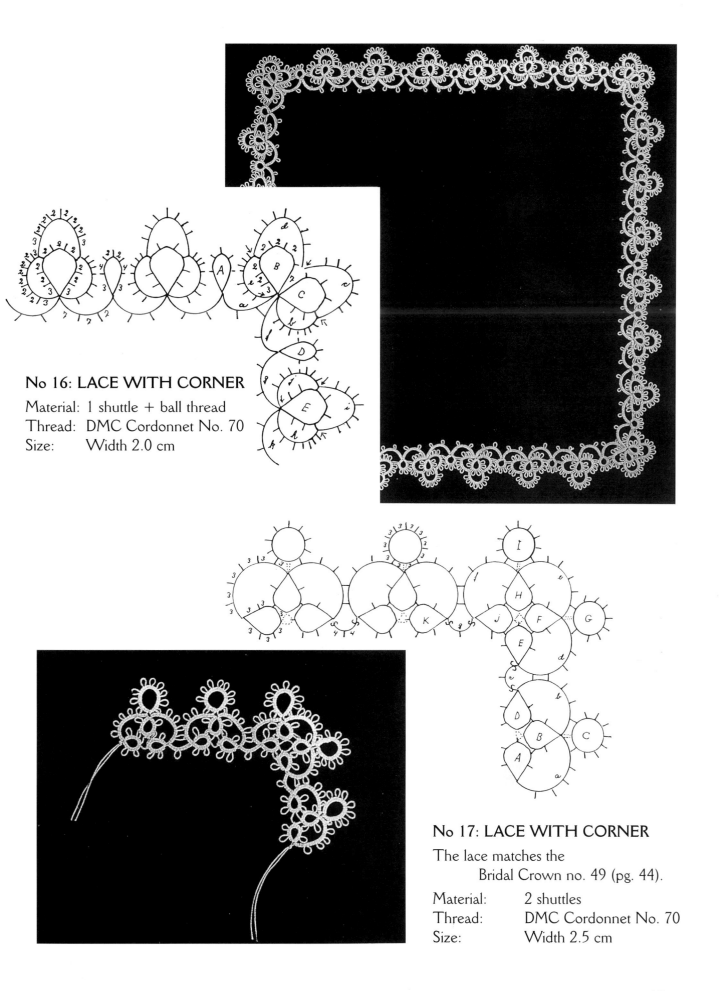

No 16: LACE WITH CORNER

Material: 1 shuttle + ball thread
Thread: DMC Cordonnet No. 70
Size: Width 2.0 cm

No 17: LACE WITH CORNER

The lace matches the
    Bridal Crown no. 49 (pg. 44).

Material: 2 shuttles
Thread: DMC Cordonnet No. 70
Size: Width 2.5 cm

No 18: LACE WITH CORNER

Notice that the corner motif is tatted on at the end.

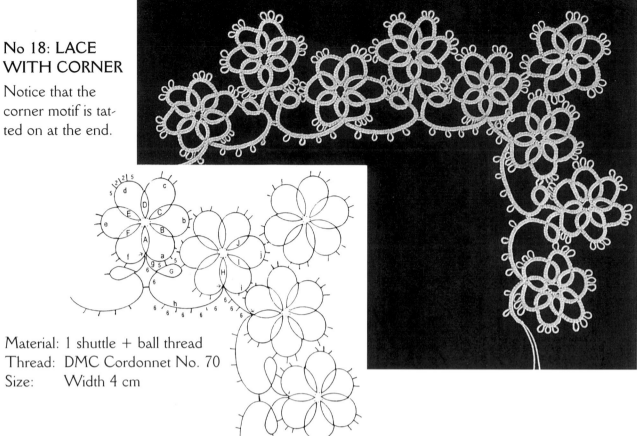

Material: 1 shuttle + ball thread
Thread: DMC Cordonnet No. 70
Size: Width 4 cm

No 19: LACE WITH CORNER

Tat the inner round. Next tat the corner motif in two rounds, i.e. first ring (A) and next all chains with the ball thread. Tat the outermost round last.

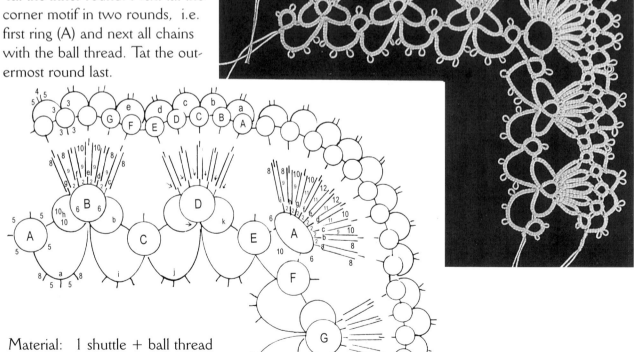

Material: 1 shuttle + ball thread
Thread: DMC Cordonnet No. 70
Size: Width 4 cm

No 20: LACE WITH CORNER

The innermost round is tatted first. Then tat the triangular corner motif and finally the outermost round.

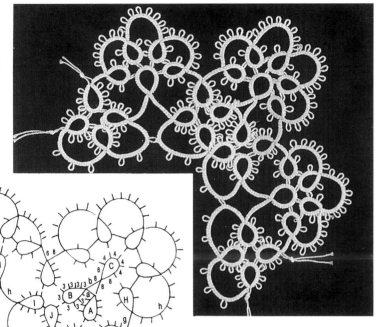

Material: 1 shuttle + ball thread
Thread: DMC Cordonnet No. 70
Size: Width 4.5 cm

No 21: LACE WITH CORNER

Notice that the corner motif is tatted on at the end.

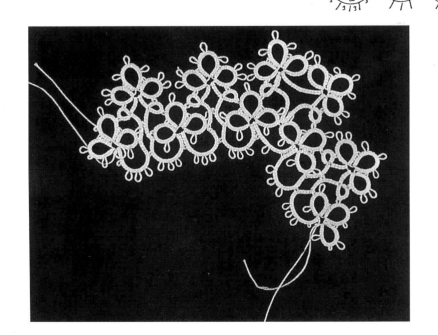

Material: 1 shuttle + ball thread
Th read: DMC Cordonnet No. 70
Size: Width 3.5 cm

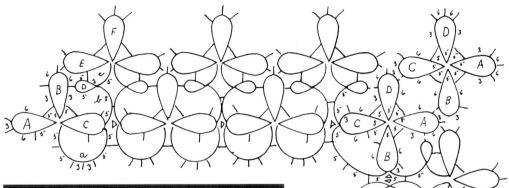

No 22: LACE WITH CORNER

The lace is the same as no. 21 with an additional corner. The two four-leaf clovers are tatted on one by one.

Material: 1 shuttle + ball thread
Thread: DMC Cordonnet No. 70
Size: Width 3.5 cm

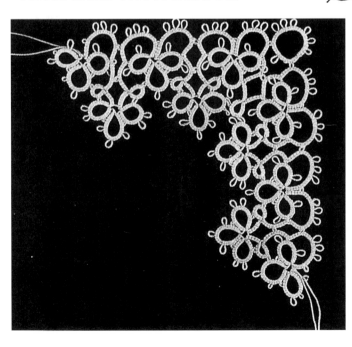

No 23: LACE WITH CORNER

This lace is the same as no. 21 and no. 22. The only difference is that the corner turns the other way, making the lace suitable as insertion in a neckline. The ring in the corner is tatted on at the end.

Material: 1 shuttle + ball thread
Thread: DMC Cordonnet No. 70
Size: Width 3.5 cm

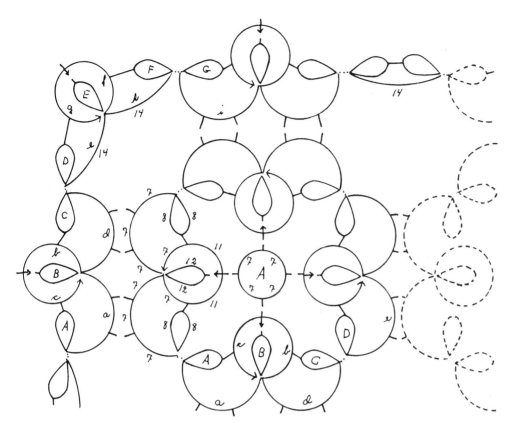

No 24: DOILY - OR BED
COVER

Material:
  1 shuttle + ball thread
Thread:
  DMC Cordonnet No. 20
Size:
  Square motif 5.5 cm in
    diameter
  Edge width 2.5 cm

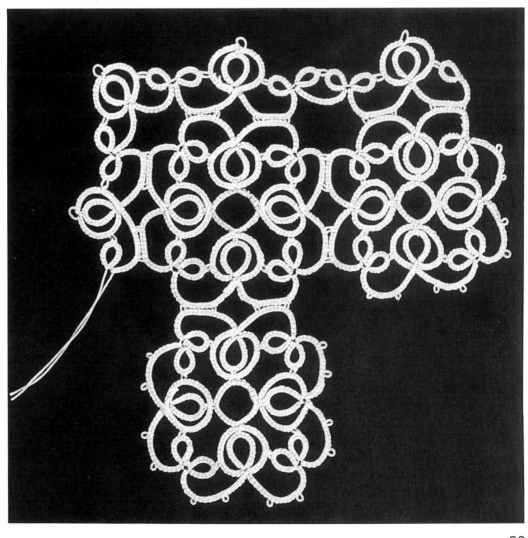

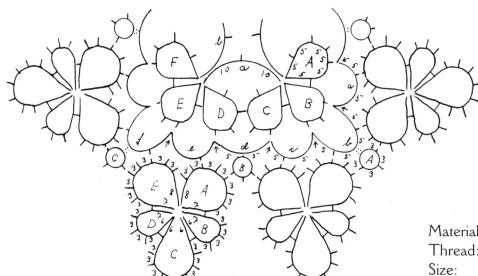

No 25: DOILY

First tat the 8 outer 5-ring motifs. Then tat the central motif with the 4 trefoils. Finally join the central motif and the outer motifs with the middle round.

Material: 2 shuttles
Thread: DMC Cordonnet No. 70
Size: Width 13 cm

No 26: DOILY

Start with the central motif. The square ring is actually a chain tatted with the ball thread; start at the paper clip.

In the outermost motif note that chain (a) is tatted on the "front side", chain (b) on the "back side" and chain (c) on the "back side." Notice how the chains are curving in the pattern.

Rings with identical letters such as D‑D indicate that both rings originate from the same place but are tatted with different shuttles.

Material: 2 shuttles
Thread: DMC Cordonnet No. 20
Size: Width 13 cm

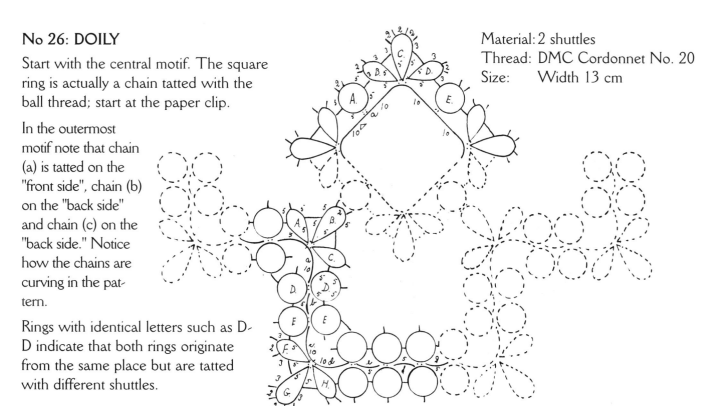

No 27: RING DOILY

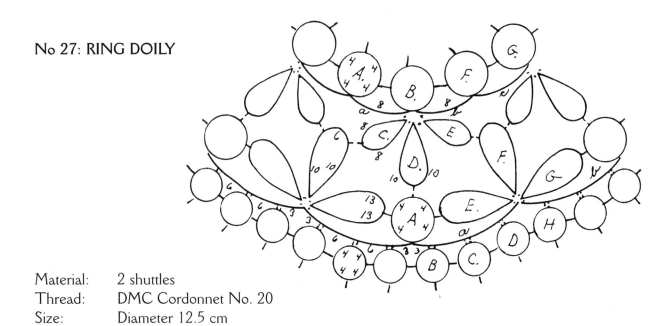

Material: 2 shuttles
Thread: DMC Cordonnet No. 20
Size: Diameter 12.5 cm

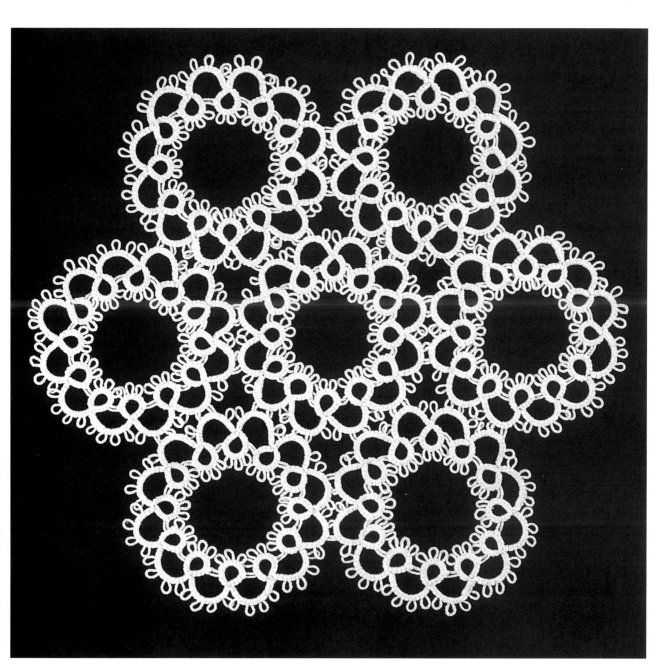

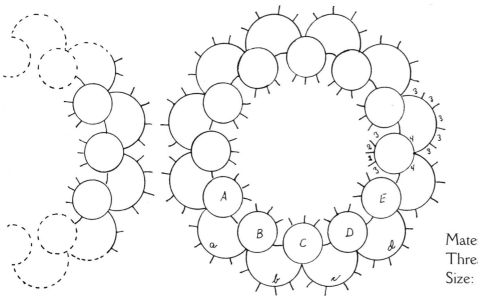

No 28: DOILY

Material: 1 shuttle + ball thread
Thread: DMC Cordonnet No. 20
Size: Diameter 16 cm

27

No 29: DOILY

Rings (B) and (C) originate from the same place. Ring (C) is tatted with the ball thread i.e. the shuttles are exchanged at ~

Material: 2 shuttles
Thread: DMC Cordonnet No. 20
Size: Diameter 16 cm

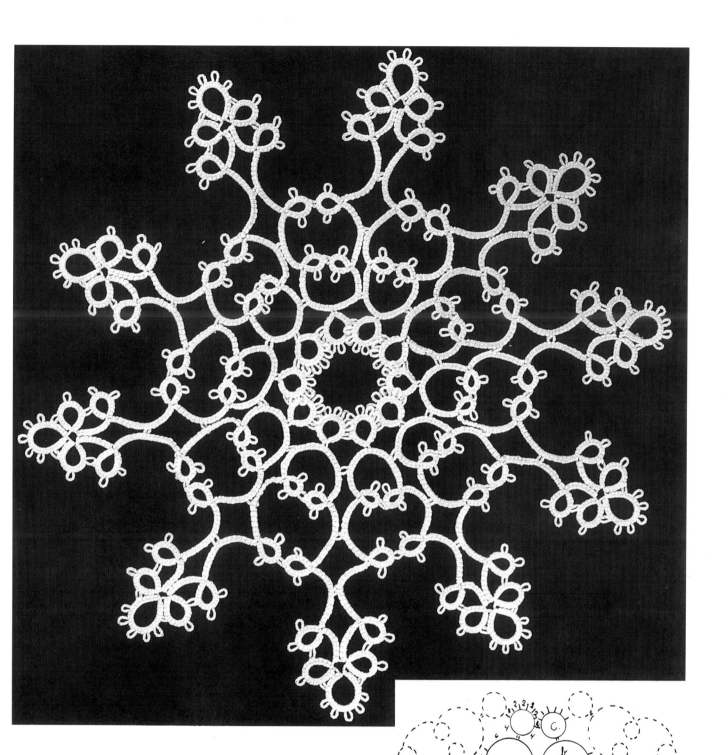

No 30: STAR DOILY

Material: 2 Shuttles
Thread: DMC Cordonnet No. 20
Size: Diameter 18 cm

No 31: DOILY

The doily is made of motifs consisting of one large flower and parts of several small flowers. The small flowers will first become visible when the motifs are joined.

When the desired size is reached the work is finished with the outermost round completing all the small flowers.

Material:	2 shuttles
Thread:	DMC Cordonnet No. 20
Size:	Diameter 21 cm

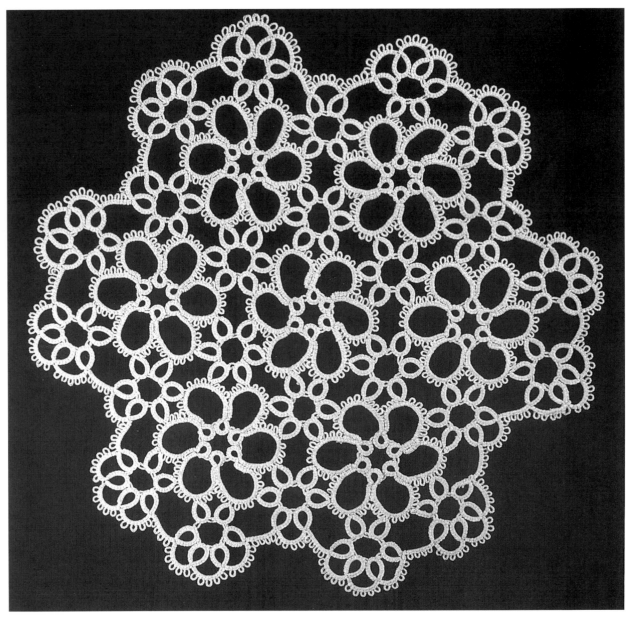

30

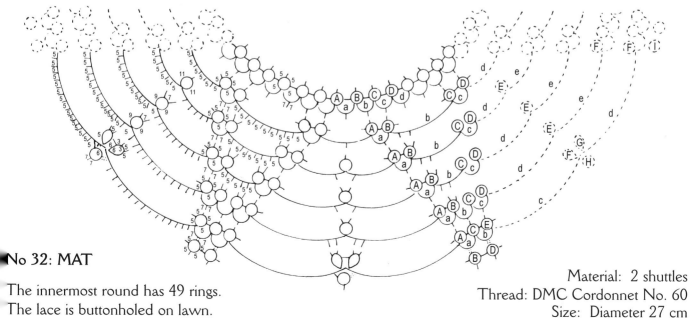

No 32: MAT

The innermost round has 49 rings.
The lace is buttonholed on lawn.

Material: 2 shuttles
Thread: DMC Cordonnet No. 60
Size: Diameter 27 cm

31

No 33: MAT

For clarity there are only a few figures on this diagram. There are 3 double stitches between each picot.

Material: 2 shuttles
Thread: DMC Cordonnet No. 20
Size: Diameter 27 cm

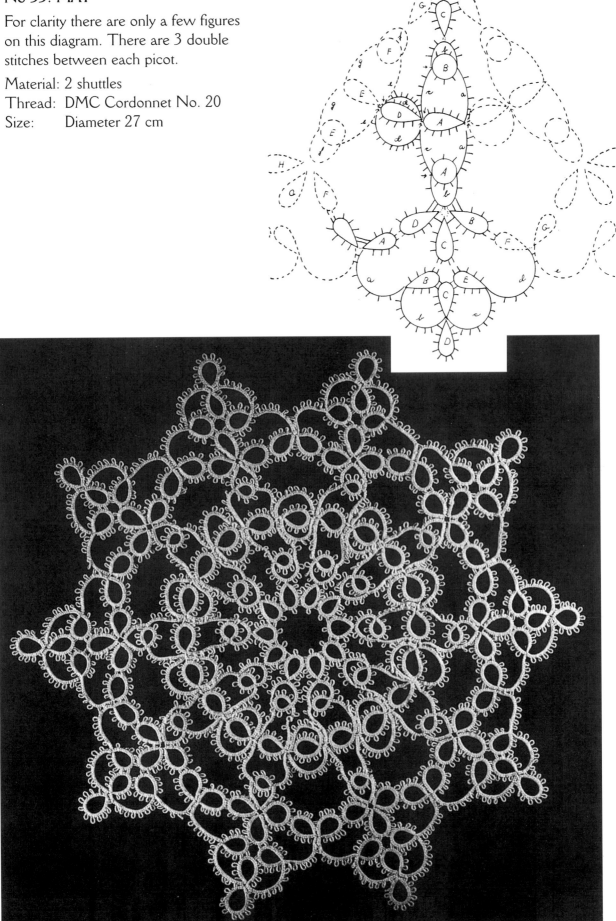

No 34: MAT

For clarity there are only a few figures on this diagram. There are 3 double stitches between each picot.

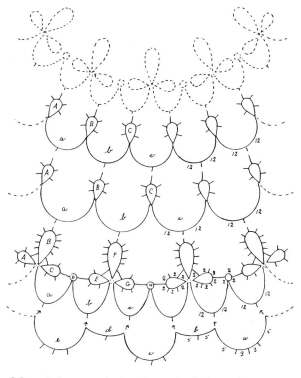

Material:	1 shuttle + ball thread
Thread:	DMC Cordonnet No. 20
Size:	Length 37 cm
	Width 29 cm

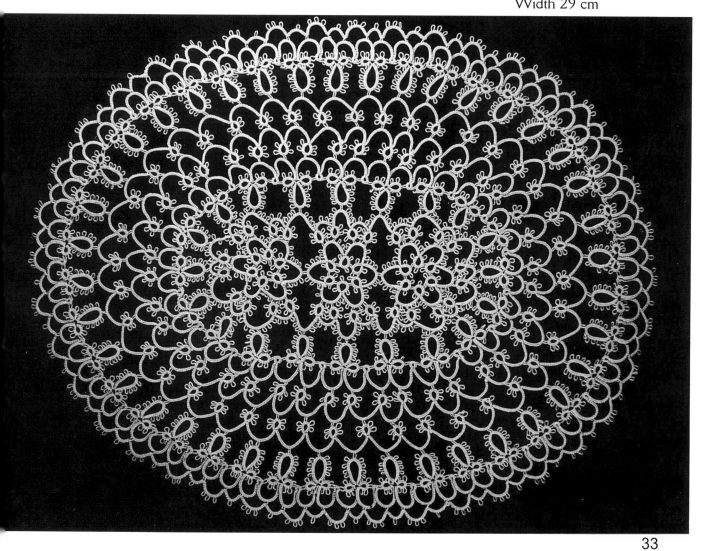

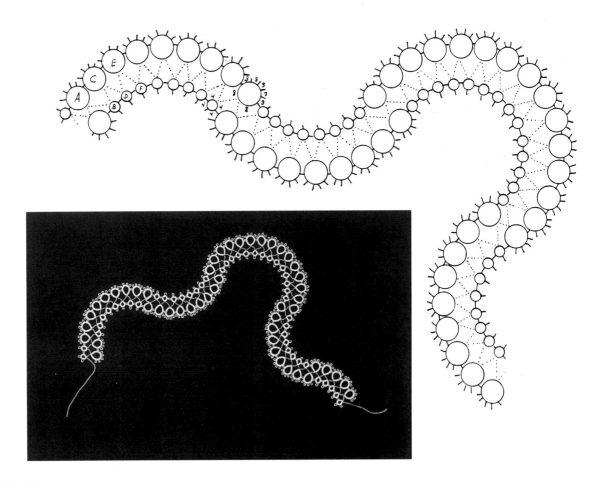

No 35: INSERTION

The work is turned between each ring.

Material: 1 shuttle
Thread: DMC Cordonnet No. 70
Size: Width 2 cm

No 36: INSERTION

Material: 1 shuttle + ball thread
Thread: DMC Cordonnet No. 20
Size: Width 3 cm

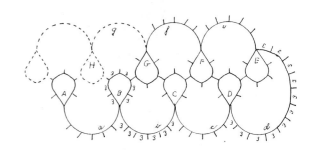

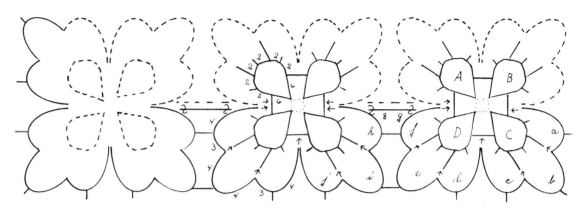

No 37: INSERTION

All four-leaf clovers are tatted first. When the desired number are completed they are joined with the outermost round which is all chains.

Material: 2 shuttles
Thread: DMC Cordonnet No. 50
Size: Width 2.5 cm

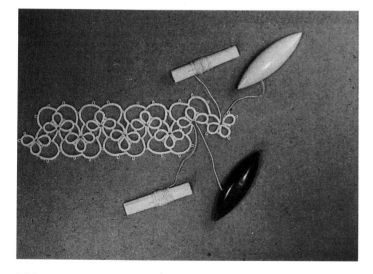

No 38: INSERTION

2 shuttles and 2 ball threads are used at the same time.

With first shuttle tat the trefoil A, B, C. Next tat with the second shuttle + ball thread a, b, D, E, F. Change to the first shuttle + ball thread and tat c, d, e, f, G, H, I. Change to the second shuttle and tat g, h, i, j and the trefoil.

Material: 2 shuttles + 2 ball threads
Thread: DMC Cordonnet No. 20
Size: Width 4.5 cm

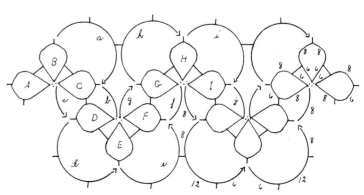

No 39: INSERTION

Start with a paper clip and tat the chain (a).
Turn the work and tat the ring (A) and join
it with the chain where the paper clip was.

Material: 1 shuttle + ball thread
Thread: DMC Cordonnet No. 70
Size: Width 5 cm

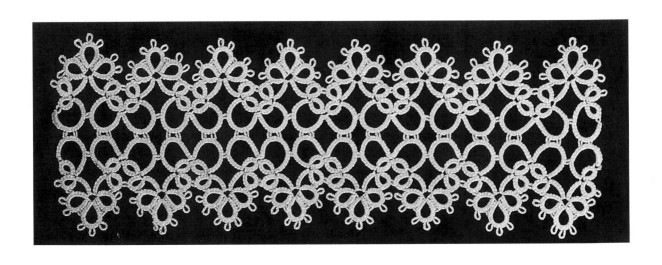

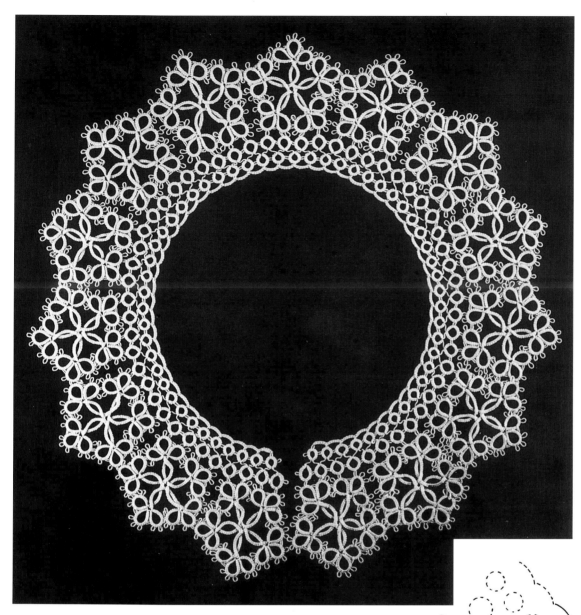

No 40: COLLAR

Material: 1 shuttle + ball thread
Thread: DMC Cordonnet No. 40
Size: Approx. 40 cm around the neck
           Width 6.5 cm

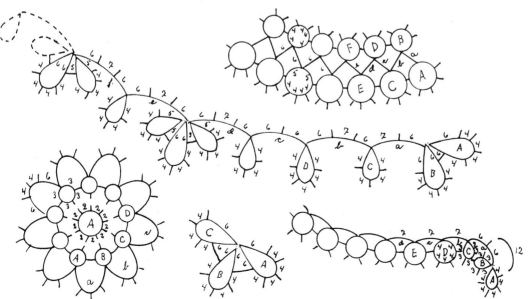

No 41: COLLAR

The wheels are tatted and joined. There are a total of 27. Next tat the trefoil motifs and finally the 3 rows. The places to join appear on the diagram. End the work with a "buttonhole" made of a small chain between two picots.

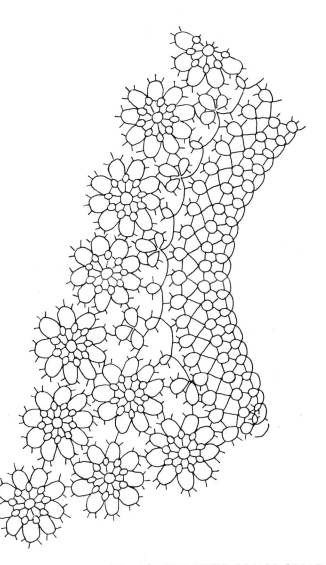

No 42: PLEATED WAX GUARD

Before the work is started thread 12 beads on the second shuttle thread.

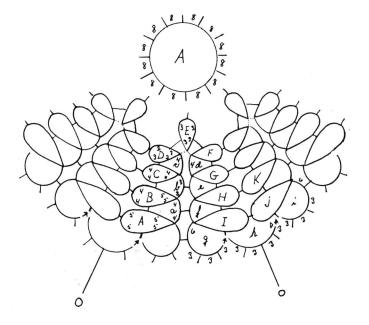

Material:	1 shuttle + ball thread
Thread:	DMC Cordonnet No. 70
Size:	39 cm around the neck.
	Width 6 cm at the back of the neck

Pull a bead forward to the middle on chain (h) and decide the length of the string.

Hold onto the bead and tat left stitches back to the chain. The string which the bead is hanging in will now appear twisted. Now finish the chain (h).

The innermost round is tatted at the end.

When the wax guard is finished stiffen and pleat it.

Material:	2 shuttles
Thread:	DMC Cordonnet No. 40
Size:	Width 3.5 cm

No 43: WAX GUARD

For clarity there are only a few figures on this diagram. Where the figures are missing there are 3 double stitches between each picot. Before the work is started thread 36 beads on the first shuttle thread.

After completing chain (b) turn the work and put in a paper clip before ring (B) is tatted with first shuttle. Next exchange the shuttles and tat chain (c) on the same side.

Remember to pull a bead forward. Then tat chain (c), put in a paper clip, exchange the shuttles and turn the work and tat chain (d). The innermost round is tatted at the end.

Material: 2 shuttles
Thread: DMC Cordonnet No. 40
Size: Width 5 cm

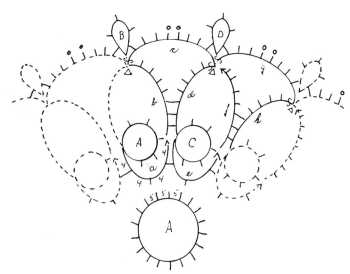

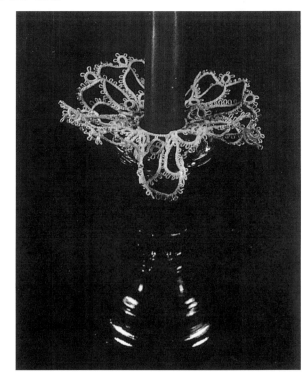

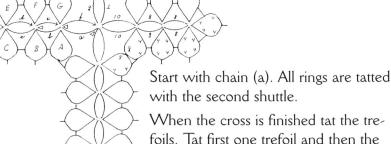

No 44: BOOKMARK - CROSS

Start with chain (a). All rings are tatted with the second shuttle.

When the cross is finished tat the trefoils. Tat first one trefoil and then the strings as one long chain. The chain is tatted with left half knots only giving it the twisted appearance.

Material: 2 shuttles
Thread: DMC Cordonnet No. 40
Size: Length 8.5 cm
          Width 6 cm

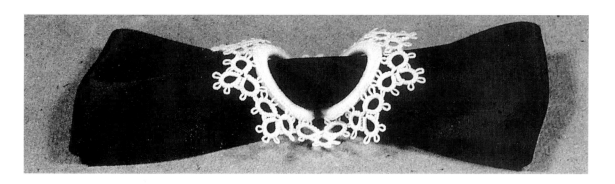

No 45: HAIR BOW ORNAMENT

There is double crochet around two thin curtain rings which measure 1.8 cm in diameter.

The rings are sewn together for approximately 1 cm so they make an angle.

The 10 trefoils are tatted one by one and gradually joined into a ring. When completed the work is sewn to the curtain rings with a thin sewing thread.

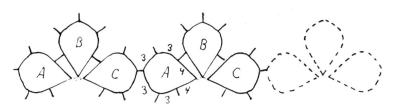

Material: 1 shuttle
Thread: DMC Cordonnet No. 70
Size: Trefoil height 1.3 cm
            Trefoil length 1.8 cm

No 46: HAIR BOW ORNAMENT

Join the thread on the two shuttles and wind sufficient thread from one shuttle to the other so that the whole flower can be made without adding additional thread.

The thread is not cut when the ring is tatted but the shuttles are exchanged so that the chains are tatted on the same side.

Put in a paper clip when the first chain is started.

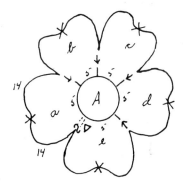

Material: 2 shuttles
Th read: DMC Cordonnet No. 40
Size: Flower diameter approx. 3 cm

No 47: BRIDAL HEADPIECE WITH BEADS

Before the top edge is tatted place 68 beads on
the ball thread.

Material: 1 shuttle + ball thread
Thread: DMC Cordonnet No. 20
Size: Height, 4.5 cm
            Length, 6 motifs = 19 cm
                     along bottom edge.

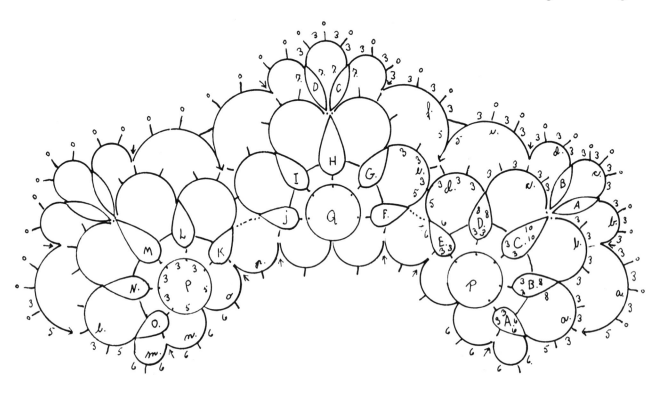

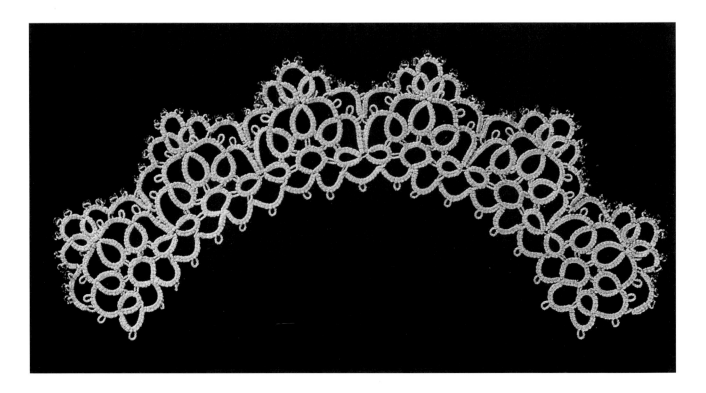

No 48: BRIDAL CROWN

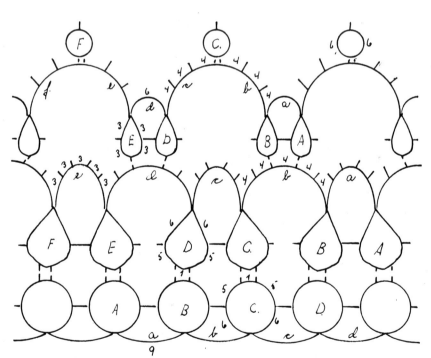

The bottom edge has 16 rings.

Material: 2 shuttles
Thread: DMC No. 5 Pearl Cotton
Size: Height 7 cm.
              Circumference 22 cm along bottom edge

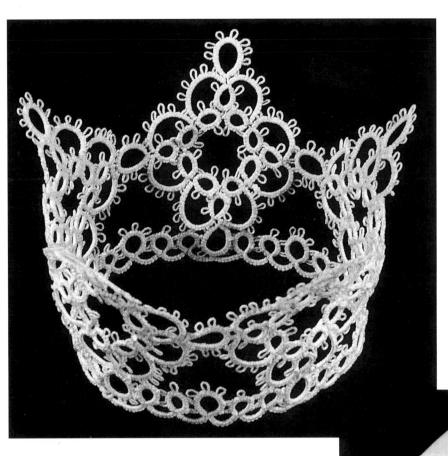

No 49: BRIDAL CROWN

The bridal crown matches the lace in design No. 17.

The crown is made of 5 motifs, plus a bottom edge.

The figures on the pattern are omitted because there are 3 double stitches between each picot except in the bottom round.

Material: 2 shuttles
Thread: DMC Cordonnet No. 20
Size: Height 7.5 cm
        Circumference 26 cm
          along bottom edge

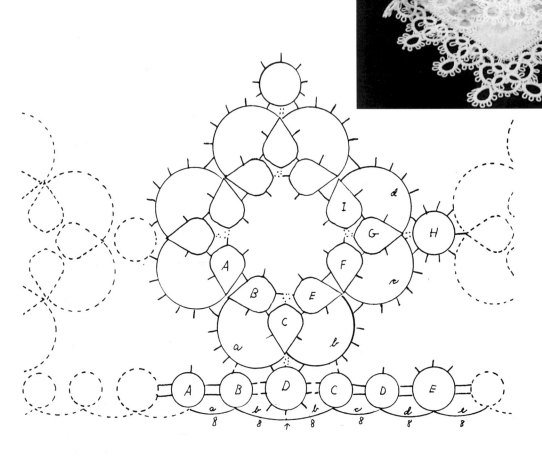

No 50: GARTER

Tat ring (A). Put in a paper clip, exchange shuttles and tat chain (a) on the same side. Turn the work. Tat ring (B), exchange shuttles and tat chain (b) on the same side. Turn work, tat ring (C) and exchange shuttles before tatting chain (c).

Finish by threading an elastic and a silk ribbon through center chains.

Material: 2 shuttles
Thread: DMC Cordonnet No. 50
Size: Width 3.5 cm

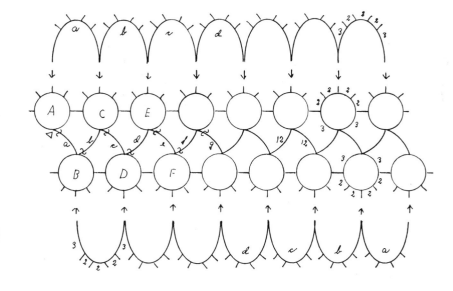

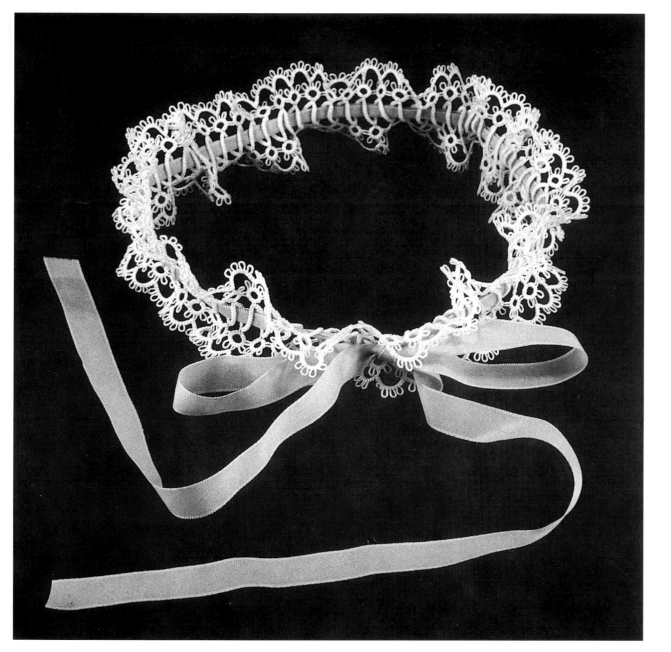

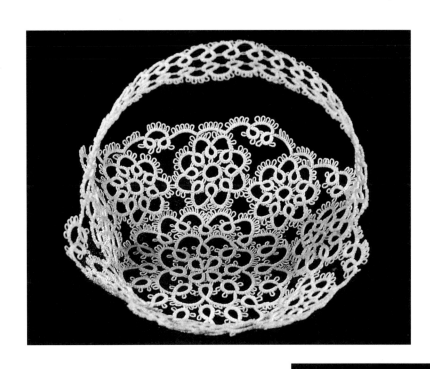

No 51: BASKET

The bottom is made of 3 rows; the sides are made of 8 wheels and a top edge.

The handle is made of 20 rings.

Material: 1 shuttle + ball thread
Thread: DMC Cordonnet No. 20
Size: Bottom: Diameter 8.5 cm
           Sides: Height 4.5 cm
           Handle: Length 20 cm

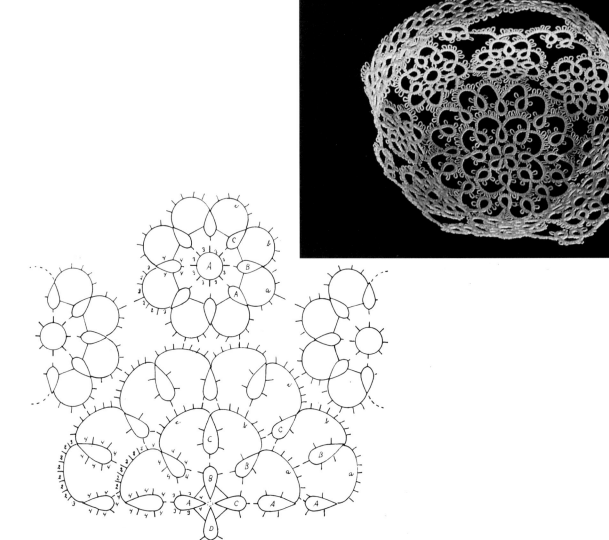

No 51: BASKET (Continued)

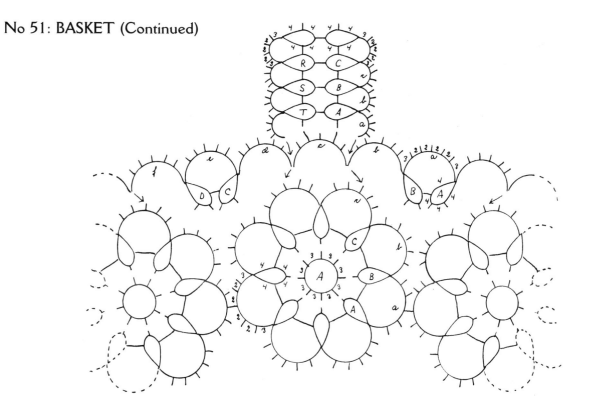

No 52: LACE EDGING FOR BRIDAL VEIL

Made entirely of chains

Material: 2 shuttles
Thread: DMC Cordonnet No. 70
Size: Width approx. 1.5 cm

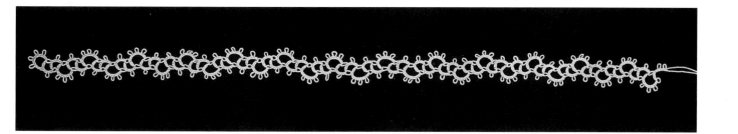

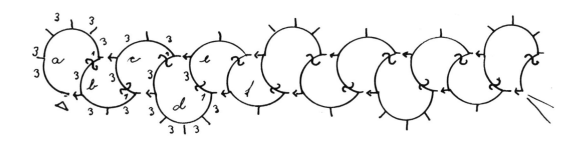

BIBLIOGRAPHY

A selection of international publications conveying tatting patterns, most in the universal charted language:

BEADS IN TATTING. Judith Connors. *Techniques for adding sparkle to any tatting pattern. Visual diagrams and a good variety of projects.* 1997, Lacis

BRIDAL TATTING, Alice Heim. *Projects to accent a wedding.* 1992, DMC

THE COMPLETE BOOK OF TATTING, Rebecca Jones. *Detailed instructions for 5 basic methods of tatting with patterns and projects for both beginner and expert. All designs charted for ease of working. Offers in-depth instruction for Needle Tatting. A must for any tatter.* 1992, Lacis

FESTIVE TATTING, DMC. *A beginner's guide to tatting with diagrams and instructions for a variety of holiday ornaments.* 1983, DMC

LEARN NEEDLE TATTING, STEP BY STEP, Barbara Foster. *The most complete step-by-step instructions for Needle Tatting.* 1998, Handy Hands

NEW DIMENSIONS IN TATTING, To de Haan-van Beek. *Pictorial tatting using color, reverse picots and layering.* 1994, Lacis

OCCHI SCHIFFCHENSPITZE, Burda. *A collection of contemporary tatting projects, each described by photo and chart. German text.* 1998, Augustus Verlag

PRACTICAL TATTING, Phyllis Sparks. *Collars, mats and edgings by photos and diagrams. 33 new patterns for shuttle or needle.* 1993, Lacis

PRETTY TATTING LACE ARTICLES, Sumi Fujishige. *Projects include collars, ornaments, borders, and flowers using Cordonnet and Cebelia, sizes 20-40. Clear step by step instructions by picture and drawing. All patterns by graphic description. Japanese text.* 1998, Nihon Vogue

TATTED LACE OF BEADS, THE TECHNIQUES OF BEANILE LACE, Nina Libin. *Tatting with beads transformed into an art form through the innovative approach of the author in manipulating thread and bead. Patterns graphically presented.* 1998, Lacis

TATTING, DMC. *Detailed tatting instructions and close up photographs for traditional lace motifs, insertions, edgings, etc.* 1987, DMC

TATTING & BEAD TATTING 1 (9401) & 2 (9505), Mituko Ikuta. *Fully illustrated with innovative bead techniques and projects for wearables and home dec. Charted patterns, Japanese text.* 1994/1995, Japanese

TATTING COLLAGE, Lindsay Rogers. *A most innovative approach to designs in tatting, utilizing the combination of simple shapes to create free-form designs.* 1996, Guild of Master Craftsman

TATTING FOR TODAY, Marion T. Leyds. *The elegance of tatting with lace motifs, pincushion covers, collar and cuff sets, necklaces and assorted decorations.* 1980, DMC

TATTING LACE, Teiko Fujito. *Excellent diagrams and color photos demonstrate tatting patterns for a variety of items including a stunning shawl and curtain pattern. Japanese text.* 1995, Nihon Vogue

TATTING WITH VISUAL PATTERNS, Mary Konior. *A new collection of tatting patterns, each illustrated graphically and with photo, covering a wide range of skills.* 1992, Lacis

TO BOLDLY GO WHERE NO SHUTTLE HAS GONE BEFORE, Anne Dyer. *"Tatting Definitely Not for Beginners." Patterns ranging from a Saxon face to wrought iron work, using different threads from coarse to the finest silk. Novel techniques are taught to ignite the imagination.* 1993, Point Ground

THE DMC ENCYCLOPEDIA OF NEEDLEWORK. *The prime and most respected resource for virtually every needlework technique since the first edition was printed over 100 years ago.* c. 1890, DMC